MONSTER
BATTLES

Written by Julia March

Editor Pamela Afram
Project Art Editor Jon Hall
Designers Anne Sharples, Stefan Georgiou
Pre-Production Producer Siu Yin Chan
Producer Louise Daly
Managing Editor Paula Regan
Managing Art Editor Guy Harvey
Art Director Lisa Lanzarini
Publisher Julie Ferris
Publishing Director Simon Beecroft

Reading Consultant
Linda B. Gambrell, Ph.D

First American Edition, 2016
Published in the United States by DK Publishing
345 Hudson Street, New York, New York 10014

Page design copyright © 2016
Dorling Kindersley Limited
DK, a Division of Penguin Random House LLC

16 17 18 19 10 9 8 7 6 5 4 3 2 1
001–288031–March/2016

Copyright © 2016 Dorling Kindersley Limited

A catalog record for this book is available
from the Library of Congress.

DK books are available at special discounts when
purchased in bulk for sales promotions,
premiums, fund-raising, or educational use.
For details, contact: DK Publishing Special Markets,
345 Hudson Street, New York, New York 10014
SpecialSales@dk.com

ISBN: 978-1-4654-4475-2 (Hardback)
ISBN: 978-1-4654-4476-9 (Paperback)

Printed and bound in China

www.LEGO.com
www.dk.com

A WORLD OF IDEAS:
SEE ALL THERE IS TO KNOW

LEGO® NEXO KNIGHTS™: MERLOK 2.0

Free app • Kostenlose App • Appli gratuite
App gratis • App Grátis • Ingyenes alkalmazás

Device check: Gerät prüfen: Vérification du dispositif:
Comprueba tu dispositivo: Verificação do dispositivo:
Eszközellenőrzés: **LEGO.COM/devicecheck**

Each of the knights has a Shield Power
you can scan. Here is Aaron's:

There are four other scannable shields within
the pages of this book—can you find them?

Contents

Welcome to Knighton

One hundred and fifty years ago, monsters ran wild in the land of Knighton. They scared people, broke their things, and burned their houses. Why? Well, just because it was fun to mess things up!

But then Merlok came along. Merlok is the wisest, coolest wizard ever. Using his powerful magic, Merlok made every last monster disappear. Only Merlok knows for sure where they went. But some say the monsters are still around, trapped inside a magic book in Merlok's library.

Jestro vs. Merlok

Jestro does not like being a jester. He is terrible at his job. Everyone mocks him. If only he could find something he is really good at.

Jestro finds a magic book called the Book of Monsters in the castle library. The book suggests something that Jestro might be good at—being bad! Just as Jestro is trying out some evil magic, the king's wizard, Merlok, discovers him. He casts a spell to stop Jestro, but the spell is so powerful the library explodes! Merlok is sucked into the castle's computer system, and Jestro and a lot of evil magic books are blown across Knighton.

THE LAND OF

THE LAVA LANDS

Burning rivers flow in The Lava Lands. Only a monster could survive here!

The King and Queen of Knighton

KNIGHTON

King and Queen Halbert are proud of their land. It has cities, villages, roads, forests, mountains, rivers, and beaches. Near the center is the royal castle.

THE CASTLE

The King and Queen rule Knighton from this towering, high-tech castle.

DARK WOOD

This dark wood is a little scary. It looks like just the place to hatch an evil plot.

Meet the Knights

Five young knights have just
graduated from Knights' Academy.
Clay wears blue and loves to train.
He also reads the Knights' Code every
day. Lance wears white and likes his
armor extra shiny! Aaron's armor
is mostly green. He loves speed,
heights, and anything else that scares
the average person silly. Big, strong
Axl wears yellow, and he is always
hungry for battle—and food! Macy
is a princess who prefers her red
armor to sparkly dresses.

These eager new knights will
soon need their battle skills.
Jestro and his monsters are
about to attack Knighton.

The Book of Monsters

Jestro wakes up on the other side
of Knighton. Nearby is the Book
of Monsters. The evil book cackles.
It is free at last! Now it can begin
making mischief, but first it needs
somebody to help release the fiery
monsters trapped within its pages.

It also needs somebody to find the
other evil magic books from the library
so it can make powerful monsters.
Jestro agrees to help
the Book of Monsters.
He plans to send
the monsters after
everyone who has
ever mocked him.
What evil fun!

Merlok 2.0

Everyone at the castle is asking "Where did Merlok go?" A smart student named Ava at the Knights' Academy discovers that the wizard is stuck inside the castle's computer system. She figures out a way to talk to him. Now that he is locked inside a computer, Merlok is known as Merlok 2.0. He has new powers that are a mixture of magic and technology. He can also upload a whole range of awesome NEXO Powers and weapons to the knights wherever they are.

The Fortrex

The NEXO KNIGHTS™ heroes will
have to travel all over Knighton to
catch Jestro and his terrible monsters.
King Halbert lends them
an amazing rolling
castle to be their
base. They name it
The Fortrex.

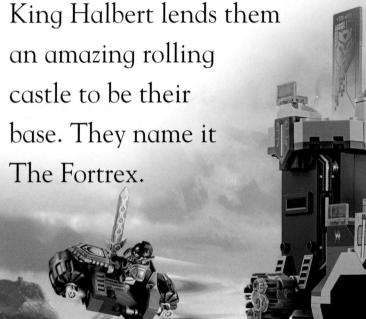

The Fortrex travels on treads,
like a tank. It has a bedroom,
an armory, a training area,
and a kitchen with a Chefbot
to prepare meals. It even
has a computer room, so the
knights can take
Merlok 2.0 with
them. They are
going to need
his help!

MAGMA MONSTERS

Here are some of the fiercest, fieriest faces in the monster army. They are hot stuff on the battlefield. Fight them at your peril!

SCURRIERS AND GLOBLINS

These tiny monsters are big trouble. Scurriers run at foes, and Globlins bounce at them.

SCARY: They are fast, there are a lot of them, and they work as a team.

NOT SO SCARY: On their own, these little guys are not so hot.

SCARY   **SCARIER**

SPARKKS

This massive monster towers over the others.

SCARY: He is very, very, very strong.

NOT SO SCARY: He is not at all smart. It is easy to outwit him.

THE BEAST MASTER

The Beast Master controls the Globlins.

SCARY: He can turn Globlins into a mass of controlled rage.

NOT SO SCARY: He cannot always control his own temper!

SCARIEST

The Evil Mobile

When Jestro sees The Fortrex,
he is jealous. Those knights think
they are so smart, cruising around
Knighton in their flashy rolling
castle! Well, Jestro can do that, too.
He summons some creatures out of
the Book of Monsters. Jestro orders
them to build him a rolling
fort of his own. He names
it the Evil Mobile.

Jestro commands
a monster named
Sparkks to tow the
Evil Mobile. Now it
is much easier for him
to roam all over Knighton
and attack different towns.

The Lava Soldiers

Watch out for Jestro's Lava Soldiers!
These three monsters are real hotshots
with their fearsome weapons.
Their yellow eyes glow with evil glee
as they take aim at the knights.
Ash Attacker and Crust Smasher
both carry sharp weapons
and wear helmets. Crust
Smasher's helmet is especially
scary, with two sharp, yellow
horns. Flame Thrower does
not wear a helmet. Perhaps
he cannot fit a helmet over
his big mohawk hairstyle!
His weapon is a lava bow
that can fire burning bolts
from long distances.

Lance's Mecha Horse

Lance rides around on a Turbo Jouster.
This cool vehicle can knock over
monster vehicles at high speed.
At the touch of a button, it also turns
into a snorting, stamping, charging
Mecha Horse! When Lance makes
the Mecha Horse rear up, those
Magma Monsters had better be fast
to dodge its big hooves.

If they dodge the hooves, they might run right onto the end of Lance's NEXO lance! And if they avoid the lance, they might get hit by the twin missiles that can be launched from the Mecha Horse's side. No wonder the sight of this steed makes monsters stampede!

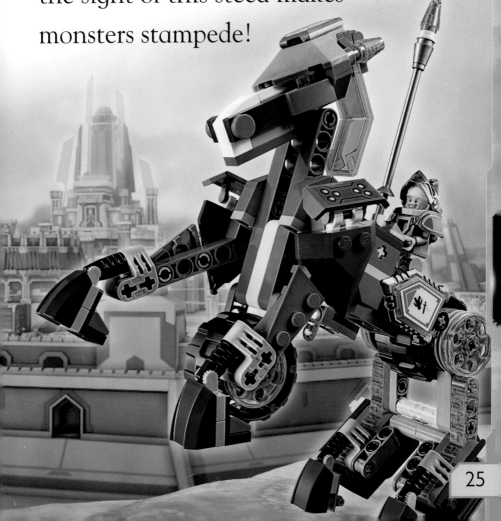

Power Upload!

To download NEXO Powers,
a knight raises his or her
NEXO Shield in the air.
Merlok 2.0 then decides
which power to upload.
Macy is being chased by
a monster. Quick as a flash, she lifts up
her shield. She feels a rush of energy,
and her shield glows as a NEXO Power
downloads. The power flows through
Macy's armor and her weapon.
What NEXO Power has Merlok 2.0
sent this time? It is the Clapper Claw!
Macy's mace fills with the power
of a mighty dragon claw. When she
swipes at a pesky monster, it is sent
back inside the Book of Monsters.

Clay's Rumble Blade

Here comes Clay, driving his
amazing Rumble Blade into battle.
The awesome vehicle has a giant
sword at the front, perfect for cutting
a path through monster armies.
From his seat in the rear cockpit,
Clay can fire missiles at oncoming foes.

If that does not stop them,
Clay has another little surprise
up his sleeve. Two small vehicles,
driven by helper Claybots, can detach
from the front of the Rumble Blade
and hurtle toward his enemies.
Monsters—get ready to rumble!

THE KNIGHTS' CODE

So you want to be a knight? Well, the first thing you must do is learn the Knights' Code. This stuff is really important, so get reading…

Be Righteous
Defend the weak, oppose the cruel, and always protect the kingdom!

Strive for Excellence
Practice your skills so you can perform to the best of your abilities.

Show Strength
Stand strong in the face of adversity.

Be Brave
Face all dangers and never give up!

Be Courteous
Carry yourself with dignity and be the best you can be.

Moltor

Moltor really rocks! In fact, he is actually made of rocks. His body is solid stone, right down to his rock-hard muscles. Nobody wants to get into a fist fight with this monster. His hands are made out of giant boulders.

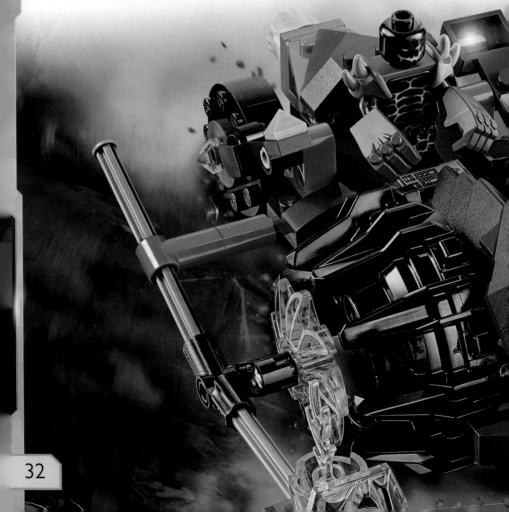

Moltor drives the Lava Smasher, which has huge rocks at the front that hammer down on his foes. The knights better not get too close to Moltor's machine. It could put some serious dents in their armor!

Battle Ready!

The knights train hard every day. They must be ready for a monster attack at any moment. Lance practices flashy moves with his lance. Aaron spends hours at target practice. He can hit the bull's-eye with bolts from his blazer bow every time.

Macy does agility training to help her wield her power mace. Axl keeps his massive muscles toned. He needs great strength to lift his heavy power ax. Clay practices his grip on his claymore sword. It is a very hard weapon to control.

The Beast Master

The Globlins are a wild bunch.
It takes an expert monster-wrangler
to control them. That's why Jestro
releases the Beast Master from
the Book of Monsters!

The Beast Master is a fierce
boss. He drags two of the wildest
Globlins around on chains.

Two large Globlins tow the Beast Master's Chaos Chariot. It has a catapult that fires flaming Globlins right at the knights.

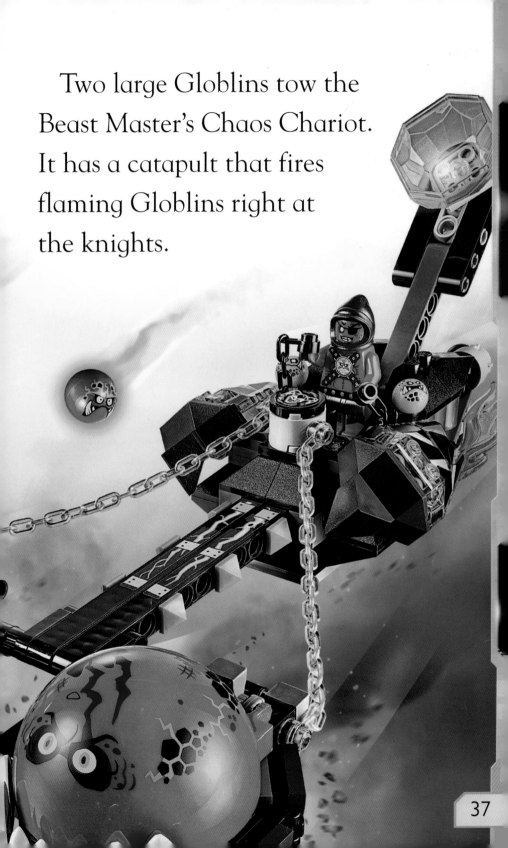

SQUIREBOTS

Even brave knights need backup. Enter the Squirebots! These little helpers do all kinds of jobs. They can be soldiers, mechanics, or musicians. There is even a Chefbot, named Chef Eclair. Each knight also has a personal Squirebot to wait on him or her and help look after their equipment.

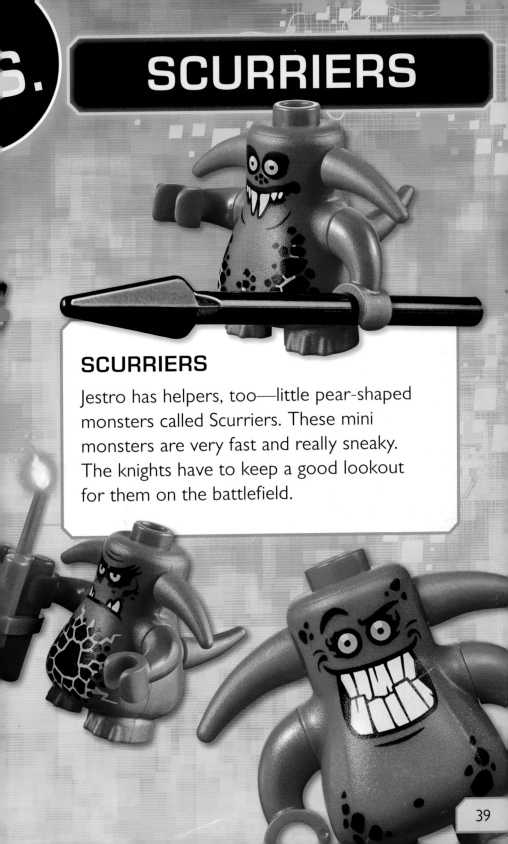

SCURRIERS

SCURRIERS

Jestro has helpers, too—little pear-shaped monsters called Scurriers. These mini monsters are very fast and really sneaky. The knights have to keep a good lookout for them on the battlefield.

The Chaos Catapult

Crazy things are happening on the battlefield. The knights are running all over the place. Why? Because Jestro and his monsters are using their Chaos Catapult.

This evil weapon fires big, burning chaos missiles at the knights. The missiles have a special power— they can make the knights forget how to work as a team. The large mouth on the front of the Chaos Catapult seems to be laughing at the knights. Come on, knights! Pull yourselves together!

NEXO
POWERS

Merlok 2.0 uploads special powers to the knights' shields to help them during a battle. Heroes, it is time to power up!

ROLLING FIRE BALL
Covers the knights with a ball of fire that damages anyone who touches it.

TOXIC STING
Releases a cloud of deadly gas. Watch out, monsters!

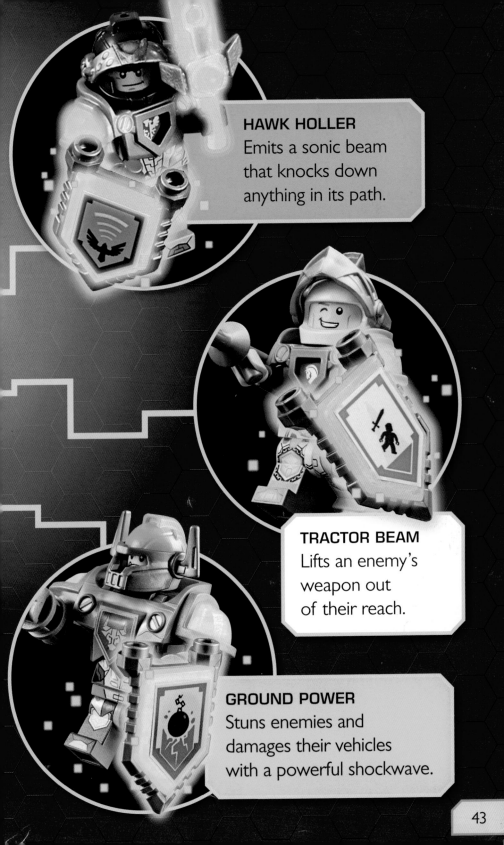

HAWK HOLLER
Emits a sonic beam that knocks down anything in its path.

TRACTOR BEAM
Lifts an enemy's weapon out of their reach.

GROUND POWER
Stuns enemies and damages their vehicles with a powerful shockwave.

Sparkks

Sparkks is the strongest
of the Magma Monsters.
But he is not as smart as
he is strong. No matter
how hard he tries, the
muscular monster always seems
to mess up on the battlefield.
The knights find it funny to think
up new ways to defeat Sparkks. He just
never seems to learn from his mistakes.
Jestro sometimes wants to get rid
of Sparkks, but he cannot do that.
Sparkks is the only monster
strong enough to tow his
Evil Mobile.

MACY'S WORLD

Home   **Contacts**   **Friends**

ABOUT ME

Name: Macy Halbert

I am an awesome knight (who just happens to be a princess). I love comic books and armor. I don't like royal balls!

Previous Posts

★ **Ball Gowns vs. Battle Armor**

★ **Squirebots**

★ **Knight Training**

★ **My Power Mace**

📷 **Photos**

Comments:

Clay
You were fantastic today, Macy!

Princess Problems

Posted: Today

Best thing about today: We had our big party in Knighton. Knight training is over. Woo-hoo!

Worst thing about today: Dad does not want me to be a knight. He says I might get hurt. He gave Clay, Lance, Aaron, and Axl shields to show they are proper knights. But not me. How unfair! I managed to grab Mom's old shield instead. She understands that I can be a knight *and* a princess. I just have to convince my Dad!

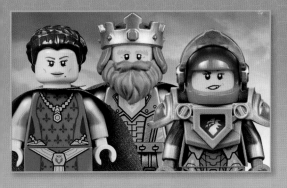

This is me and my parents at the party. I am looking grumpy because my Dad would not give me a shield!

Knighton Battle Blaster

King Halbert has Royal Soldiers that
also help to protect Knighton. The
Royal Soldiers do not have NEXO
Powers. When monsters attack, they
rely on standard battle skills—and
the Knighton Battle Blaster.

This speedy vehicle is open-sided
so the soldier can swing his sword.
Monsters running from the Battle
Blaster are careful to dodge the two
orange axes at the front. But they may
not notice the disk missile launchers.
That is, until it is too late. Ouch!

King Halbert

King Halbert does not like fighting. But soon he will have to fight. Sneaky Jestro tricks the knights into splitting up. Then his monsters capture them, one by one.

Jestro marches his monsters to the castle. With the knights out of the way, it will be easy to defeat King Halbert. Then Jestro will be king. He will make life hard for the people of Knighton. Ha ha!

Jestro thinks King Halbert will
be easy to defeat. He is wrong!
King Halbert comes out fighting.
The king has an awesome Mech Suit
with a large sword.

KING HALBERT'S MECH

Gripping hand

King Halbert's NEXO Shield

Missile-deflecting sword

King Halbert's Mech Suit is packed with high-tech gadgets and weapons. It even has a detachable shield that doubles as a small fighter jet for a helper Kingsbot to fly!

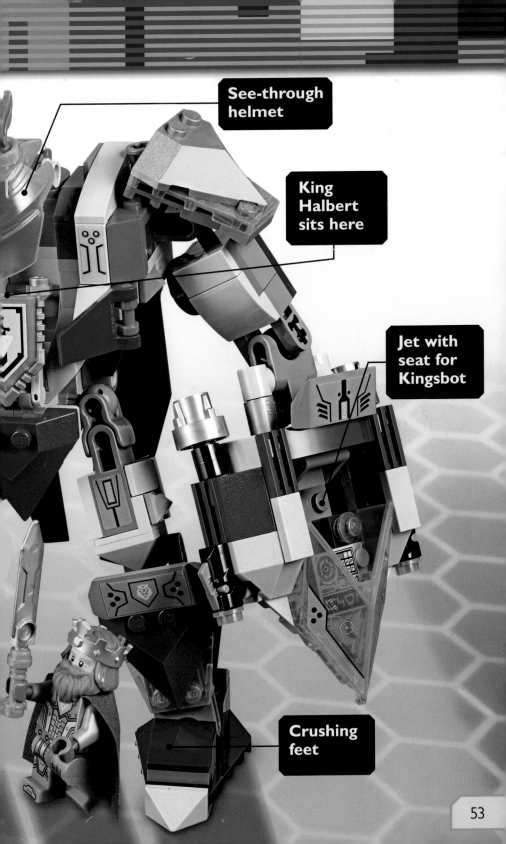

See-through helmet

King Halbert sits here

Jet with seat for Kingsbot

Crushing feet

Monster Battle

King Halbert cannot fight off the monsters forever. Where are those knights? Aaron has escaped from the monster who caught him. He rides his hovershield around Knighton, freeing the other knights. They jump into The Fortrex and head for the castle. Monsters, get ready for an epic battle!

The knights charge at the monsters. Crack! Macy's mace shatters a monster's weapon. Swish! Aaron jumps onto The Fortrex's Aero-Striker and fires at Jestro's Evil Mobile from the sky. The knights keep attacking. They do not stop until Jestro and his monsters run away.

U-Knighted!

The knights have saved the kingdom of Knighton. What a team! All over Knighton, cheers ring out for King Halbert, Merlok 2.0, and the brave knights. They have chased off Jestro and the mean monsters. But the monsters will not stay away forever. The knights will have to battle them again someday.

The people of Knighton are not worried. Now that the knights know how to work together, they should be able to beat them. Three cheers for the heroes!

Quiz

1. What color armor does Clay wear?

2. Where does Jestro find the Book of Monsters?

3. What is Macy's last name?

4. Who controls the Globlins?

5. Which Lava Soldier has a mohawk hairstyle?

6. How many rules are there in the Knights' Code?

7. Who drives the Lava Smasher?

8. Who uploads NEXO Powers
   to the knights?

9. Which monsters are Jestro's helpers?

10. Who tows Jestro's Evil Mobile?

Answers on page 61

Glossary

Adversity
A difficult situation.

Armory
A place where weapons are kept.

Claymore
A very large, two-edged sword.

Graduated
Successfully completed a course of study.

Overshield
Aaron's NEXO shield when he is riding it like a hoverboard.

Jester
A servant of a king or queen whose job is to amuse people.

Lava
Melted rock that has come out from a volcano.

Magma
Melted rock under the Earth's surface.

Mech
Mechanical

Technology
Machines created by people to make it easier to do things.

Index

Answers to the quiz on pages 58 and 59:
1. Blue 2. Merlok's library 3. Halbert
4. The Beast Master 5. Flame Thrower 6. Five
7. Moltor 8. Merlok 2.0 9. Scurriers 10. Sparkks
Scannable shields can be found on pages 2, 30,
47, 52, and 59.

Guide for Parents

DK Readers is a four-level interactive reading adventure series for children, developing the habit of reading widely for both pleasure and information. These books have an exciting main narrative interspersed with a range of reading genres to suit your child's reading ability, as required by the Common Core State Standards. Each book is designed to develop your child's reading skills, fluency, grammar awareness, and comprehension in order to build confidence and engagement when reading.

Ready for a *Reading Alone* book
YOUR CHILD SHOULD

- be able to read most words without needing to stop and break them down into sound parts.
- read smoothly, in phrases and with expression. By this level, your child will be mostly reading silently.
- self-correct when some word or sentence doesn't sound right.

A Valuable and Shared Reading Experience

For some children, text reading, particularly nonfiction, requires much effort, but adult participation can make this both fun and easier. So here are a few tips on how to use this book with your child.

TIP 1 Check out the contents together before your child begins:

- Invite your child to check the blurb, contents page, and layout of the book and comment on it.
- Ask your child to make predictions about the story.
- Talk about the information your child might want to find out.

TIP 2 Encourage fluent and flexible reading:

- Support your child to read in fluent, expressive phrases, making full use of punctuation and thinking about the meaning.

- Encourage your child to slow down and check information where appropriate.

TIP 3 Indicators that your child is reading for meaning:
- Your child will be responding to the text if he/she is self-correcting and varying his/her voice.
- Your child will want to talk about what he/she is reading or is eager to turn the page to find out what will happen next.

TIP 4 Share and discuss:
- Encourage your child to recall specific details after each chapter.
- Provide opportunities for your child to pick out interesting words and discuss what they mean.
- Discuss how the author captures the reader's interest, or how effective the nonfiction layouts are.
- Ask questions about the text. These help develop comprehension skills and awareness of the language used.

A FEW ADDITIONAL TIPS
- Read to your child regularly to demonstrate fluency, phrasing, and expression; to find out or check information; and for sharing enjoyment.
- Encourage your child to reread favorite texts to increase reading confidence and fluency.
- Check that your child is reading a range of different types of material, such as poems, jokes, and following instructions.

- Series consultant, **Dr. Linda Gambrell**, Distinguished Professor of Education at Clemson University, has served as President of the National Reading Conference, the College Reading Association, and the International Reading Association. She is also reading consultant for the **DK Adventures**.

Have you read these other great books from DK?

READING ALONE ③

© 2016 The LEGO Group

© 2015 Lucasfilm Ltd and ™

Test what makes rockets fly. Which design would you use?

Discover the new tribes threatening Chima™ with their icy powers.

Join the heroes of the rebellion as they continue to fight the Empire.

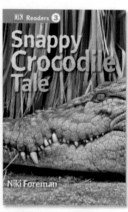

© 2016 The LEGO Group © 2016 DC Comics

© 2016 Lucasfilm Ltd and ™

Follow Chris Croc's adventures from a baby to a mighty king of the river.

Follow Batman as he fights to protect Gotham City from crime.

Buckle up and get ready for an action-packed ride!